Allstar Hockey Activity Book

- for -
Ruth
and
Jesse

ALLSTAR HOCKEY ACTIVITY BOOK

Noah and Julian Ross

POLESTAR
BOOK PUBLISHERS

Published by
Polestar Press Ltd., R.R. 1, Winlaw, B.C., VOG 2JO, 604-226-7670

Distributed by
Raincoast Books, 112 East 3rd Avenue, Vancouver, B.C., V5T 1C8, 604-873-6581

Canadian Cataloguing in Publication Data
Ross, Noah, 1982–
Allstar hockey activity book
ISBN 0-919591-60-4
1. Hockey — Miscellanea. I. Ross, Julian,
1952–   II. Title.
GV847.25.R68 1990   j.796.962   C90-091588-9

Acknowledgements
Cover design and illustration by Jim Brennan
Stanley Cup photograph by Bob Mummery
Interior illustrations by Anne Degrace
Typeset by Woodward Associates

Thanks to Netty and Tammy Zarchikoff for the Soviet hockey cards,
and to Nick Verigin for translating them.

Photographs courtesy of Bob Mummery

The authors would like to thank Jim Brennan, Anne Degrace, Ron Hearnden,
Meredith and Ron Woodward, Ruth and Jesse Ross, Kate Walker, and everyone at
Stanton & MacDougall/Raincoast.

Printed and bound in Canada by Gagne Printers

Printed on paper
containing over 50%
recycled paper including
5% post-consumer fibre.

Use a pencil for the quizzes and puzzles — you'll be able to do them again, or
challenge a friend, parent, brother or sister.

CONTENTS

NICKNAMES

Match the nicknames of the players on the left with their real names on the right.

Flower	Wayne Gretzky
Tiger	Larry Robinson
Steamer	Terry Sawchuk
Hammer	Mark Messier
Rocket	Yvan Cournoyer
The Great One	Frank Brimsek
Grapes	Richard Brodeur
Mr. Hockey	Dave Schultz
Boom Boom	Rick Middleton
Pocket Rocket	Glen Sather
Big Bird	Guy Lafleur
Rat	Stan Smyl
Road Runner	Dave Williams
Mr. Zero	Garry Unger
Mr. Zero (the original)	Gordie Howe
Slats	Maurice Richard
Nifty	Henri Richard
Mess	Bernie Geoffrion
King Richard	Don Cherry
Ironman	Ken Linseman

OPPOSITE PAGE *Guy Lafleur in his early days as a Canadien.*

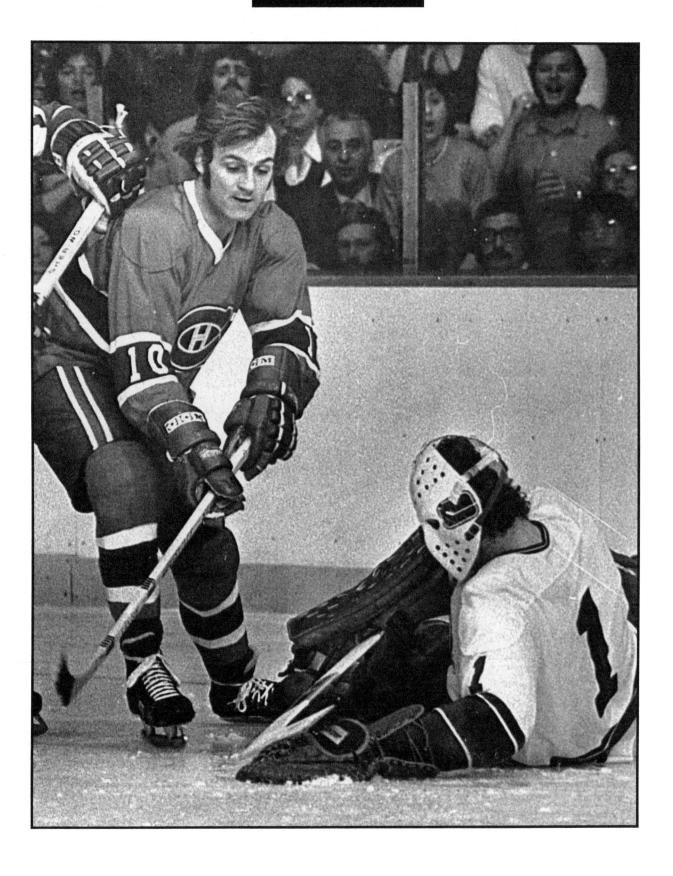

ARE YOU KIDDING?

1 Hockey pucks are made from:

- ❑ a) petrified chocolate
- ❑ b) black licorice
- ❑ c) rubber

2 The centre ice line is always coloured:

- ❑ a) red
- ❑ b) blue
- ❑ c) white

3 In a home game between Quebec and Hartford, upset fans showered the ice with:

- ❑ a) their shoes
- ❑ b) toilet paper rolls
- ❑ c) doughnuts

4 One of the most famous hockey announcers was:

- ❑ a) Howie Morenz
- ❑ b) Bo Jackson
- ❑ c) Foster Hewitt

5 Hockey is quite similar to:

- ❑ a) Australian Rules Football
- ❑ b) lacrosse
- ❑ c) baseball

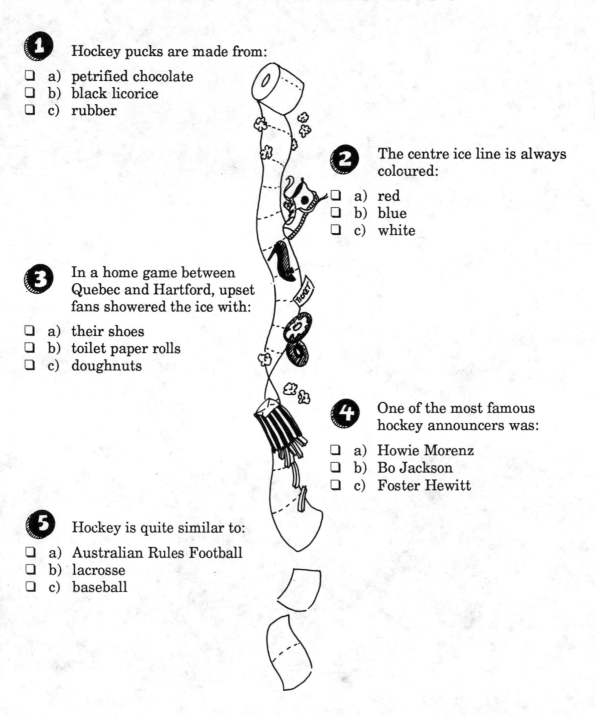

6 Hockey equipment is similar to the equipment worn by:

- ❑ a) knights
- ❑ b) rugby players
- ❑ c) mountain climbers

8 Who was the youngest player to score 50 goals in the NHL?

- ❑ a) Dale Hawerchuk
- ❑ b) Eric Lindros
- ❑ c) Wayne Gretzky

7 A Stanley Cup final game between Boston and Edmonton was postponed because:

- ❑ a) the players had to catch an early plane home
- ❑ b) the power went out and the lights went off
- ❑ c) the mosquitoes were fierce

9 Which team travelled by bike, dog team, foot, boat and train to challenge for the Stanley Cup in 1905?

- ❑ a) Moscow Dynamos
- ❑ b) Dawson Nuggets
- ❑ c) Ottawa Silver Seven

10 A World Hockey Association game was once called off because:

❑ a) the referee forgot to bring the pucks
❑ b) the zamboni crashed through the ice and sunk
❑ c) all the players on the home team went on strike

11 Who holds the record for scoring the most points in their rookie season?

❑ a) Wayne Gretzky
❑ b) Peter Stastny
❑ c) Mario Lemieux

12 Has the Stanley Cup ever been:

❑ a) kicked into a river and forgotten about for a year
❑ b) used as a flower vase in a window display
❑ c) used as a potty
❑ d) all of the above

13 At 37 years old, which Russian player became the NHL's oldest rookie?

❑ a) Sergei Makarov (Calgary)
❑ b) Viacheslav Fetisov (New Jersey)
❑ c) Helmut Balderis (Minnesota)

14 Ohio State centre David Smith scored the winning goal in overtime and his teammates rushed onto the ice to mob him. In the celebration, something awful happened. What was it?

❑ a) his pants fell down
❑ b) his leg was accidentally broken
❑ c) he got knocked out

15 Some goalies do more than stop pucks, they help score goals. Which goalie has the most points in one season?

❑ a) Grant Fuhr
❑ b) Ron Hextall
❑ c) Mike Palmateer

16 In the 1950s at Maple Leaf Gardens in Toronto, the centre red line was actually checkered. Why?

❑ a) for good luck
❑ b) because they ran out of red paint
❑ c) so it would show up on black and white television

17 Mike Keenan, the Chicago coach and general manager, has the nickname Captain Hook. Why?

❑ a) he lost his hand in an accident and wears a hook
❑ b) because of his habit of yanking goalies
❑ c) he played the role of Captain Hook in Peter Pan

WHAT A FUNNY GAME!

A Profile of Dave Elston, Hockey's #1 Humorist

Dave Elston is the kind of guy who *doesn't* take his hockey seriously. In fact, he finds it a pretty funny sport; in the last ten years he's made more than 1,000 hockey cartoons. His cartoons now appear daily in *The Calgary Sun,* weekly in *The Hockey News,* and monthly during hockey season for *Inside Hockey* magazine.

Dave, who lives in Calgary, is Canada's only full-time sports cartoonist — and hockey is his favorite sport. He started skating when he was two, playing ice hockey on outdoor rinks and road hockey during the warmer months, and he still plays wing on the Calgary media hockey team. He also started drawing when he was young, and is very pleased to be able to combine as a job two things that he enjoyed so much as a boy.

"Doing hockey cartoons is a natural thing for me," he says. "I love hockey and I love cartooning — so it's great."

But drawing cartoons isn't always an easy thing to do. "The hardest part is getting the idea, " he says. "And that can take anywhere from 15 minutes to six or eight hours." He always carries a notebook with him, and anytime he gets an idea he writes it down. To actually make the finished cartoon — which he usually does about ten times bigger than it actually appears when printed — takes between three and six hours.

How does he decide what to cartoon? "I look for what makes a person easily identifiable," he says, "what makes them stand out from everybody else. For instance, Don Cherry's clothes or Tim Hunter's nose or Theoren Fleury's height." And then he waits until the cartoons are published, and hopes that people will like them.

Usually they do. His cartoons have been featured on *Hockey Night in Canada, TSN* and regional television, and he has done customized sweatshirts and sold original cartoons to players like Lanny McDonald and Tim Hunter. He's also just had his first book published — *Elston On Ice* — a collection of 125 of his favorite hockey cartoons, and the cartoons shown here are selected from that book.

100-POINT SCORERS

```
E   S   R   E   G   O   R   Y
N   S   L   N   E   R   M   K
I   I   P   N   R   I   E   Z
A   T   B   O   S   S   Y   T
T   T   I   I   S   U   S   E
N   L   R   D   A   I   E   R
O   E   R   H   K   X   T   G
F   R   U   C   I   O   A   O
A   L   K   F   C   F   O   E
L   A   F   L   E   U   R   Y
```

Marcel DIONNE	Jari KURRI	Brett HULL	Wayne GRETZKY
Adam OATES	Darryl SITTLER	Bobby ORR	Joe SAKIC
Mike BOSSY	Mike ROGERS	Phil ESPOSITO	Pat LAFONTAINE
	Guy LAFLEUR		

We've hidden the last names of these 100-point scorers in the puzzle above.
Their names are written either forwards or backwards, and placed horizontally,
vertically or diagonally. The leftover letters, taken in order from top to bottom, spell
out the names of two current Pittsburgh Penguin all-stars!

_ _ _ _ _ _ _   _ _ _ _ _ _

WHO AM I?

This NHL defenceman was born in Czechoslovakia in 1961, but played his junior hockey in Canada. He was Vancouver's first-round draft choice in 1980, where he played for six years before being traded to Toronto. After three years in Toronto, he played a year in Switzerland before signing with Chicago for the 1990–91 season. Who is he?

GONE BUT NOT FORGOTTEN

It is a great honour for a player to have his number retired. There is often a big celebration at centre ice prior to a home game, and a large banner with the player's number is raised to the rafters to forever be remembered by fans and players alike. It also means that no other player on that team will ever wear that number again.

In total, 44 sweaters have been retired. Boston has retired the most with seven, the Canadiens have retired six, while the Islanders and the Devils are the only two teams not to have retired a number. Bobby Hull and Gordie Howe have had sweaters retired by two teams! See if you can match the retired number with the player.

Buffalo #11	Bobby Hull
Toronto #6	Lanny McDonald
St. Louis #11	Glenn Hall
Boston #4	Gilbert Perreault
Calgary #9	Bill Masterton
Detroit #9	Ace Bailey
Boston #7	Bobby Orr
Winnipeg #9	J. C. Tremblay
Chicago #35	Maurice Richard
Los Angeles #30	Guy Lafleur
Minnesota #19	Brian Sutter
Chicago #1	Phil Esposito
Montreal #10	Gordie Howe
Rangers #7	Tim Horton
Philadelphia #16	Tony Esposito
Montreal #9	Bobby Clarke
Buffalo #2	Rogatien Vachon
Quebec #3	Rod Gilbert

WHEN DID THEY START?

Match the teams on the left with the years they started in their current city on the right. For teams that have switched cities, don't worry about where they were, just where they are now. (Answers in the back.)

Boston Bruins	1979–80
Buffalo Sabres	1917–18
Calgary Flames	1974–75
Chicago Blackhawks	1979–80
Detroit Red Wings	1980–81
Edmonton Oilers	1967–68
Hartford Whalers	1970–71
Los Angeles Kings	1979–80
Minnesota North Stars	1926–27
Montreal Canadiens	1967–68
New Jersey Devils	1926–27
New York Islanders	1924–25
New York Rangers	1970–71
Philadelphia Flyers	1972–73
Pittsburgh Penguins	1967–68
Quebec Nordiques	1917–18
St. Louis Blues	1974–75
Toronto Maple Leafs	1967–68
Vancouver Canucks	1926–27
Washington Capitals	1979–80
Winnipeg Jets	1967–68

WHERE WERE THEY BORN?

In the early days of the NHL, most of the players were from Canada or the United States. But now there are players in the league from many different countries. Some teams, like the Vancouver Canucks, have players from Czechoslovakia, the Soviet Union, Sweden, Finland, Canada and the U.S. on them. In the quiz below, match these 11 players with the country they were born in.

Uwe Krupp — *Sabres;* D	Great Britain
Joe Mullen — *Penguins;* RW	France
Steve Thomas — *Hawks;* LW	Czechoslovakia
Trevor Linden — *Canucks;* C & RW	Sweden
Rod Langway — *Capitals;* D	West Germany
Peter Sidorkiewicz — *Whalers;* G	United States
Paul MacLean — *Wings;* RW	Soviet Union
Rick Lanz — *Hawks;* D	Canada
Anatoli Semenov — *Oilers;* C	Finland
Robert Nordmark — *Canucks;* D	Taiwan
Mikko Makela — *Kings;* LW	Poland

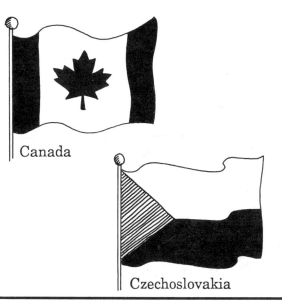

Canada

Finland

Czechoslovakia

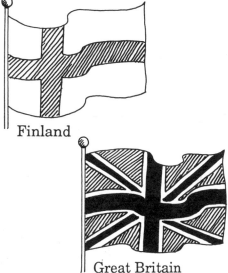

Great Britain

SOVIET STARS

Here is a special feature for all you card collectors — an exclusive look at some Soviet hockey cards!

The cards are printed in colour on a glossy, very thick card stock. They look like postcards, measure 4 1/8" tall by 5 13/16" wide, and have the player's signature in gold ink on the fronts. The backs are plain with black ink on white paper. None of the photos are game-action, and no stats are given.

We have given you exact translations from the backs of the cards.

Victor Tikhonov

Victor Tikhonov was born on June 4, 1930 in Moscow. In the 50's in the ranks of the Moscow team, Dynamo, he became a champion of the USSR four times. In 1962, Victor became a coach. From 1968 to 1977 he headed the Riga Dynamo team which in a short time advanced to being a top team.

In 1977 Tikhonov was appointed as the main coach of the Central Army team. Under his leadership the Armenian club won 12 consecutive national championships.

Tikhonov has headed the national hockey team since 1977. In this position, he has achieved great success: Soviet players were seven times world champions in Europe and twice Olympic champions in 1984 and 1988. The team has also won the Canadian Cup. Because of these and other successes, Tikhonov has gained respect and fame throughout the world.

For his outstanding success in the advancement of Soviet hockey, Victor Tikhonov has received many honours, including the Order of Lenin.

Sergei Makarov

Sergei Makarov was born on June 19, 1958 in the city of Chelyabinsk. He was raised in a family where two of his older brothers were seriously absorbed in hockey. Naturally, Sergei at an early age put on skates. In spite of his gentle character and his fascination for music, he chose sports, which demands courage and a strong will. He successfully joined the ranks of the midget and junior selected teams of the nation and was later drafted into the Central Army team.

Twice, as part of world championship teams in 1979 and 1985, he was declared the best forward, and in the 1981–82 season he was awarded the Golden Hockey Stick as the best player in Europe.

In the 1989–90 season, Makarov joined the professional NHL team, the Calgary Flames.

His country highly honors Sergei Makarov and his contribution to the development of Soviet hockey. Many awards have been bestowed upon him.

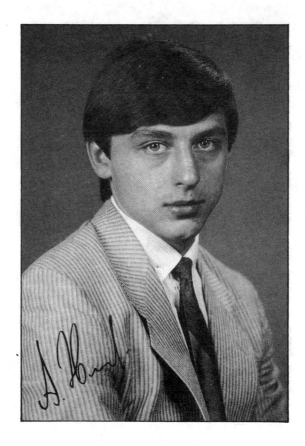

Andre Khomutov

Andre Khomutov was born on April 21, 1961 in the city of Varslav and was brought up in a sports boarding school. Khomutov at first joined a junior team and later the master Central Army team.

Andre was selected in 1980 at the time of the Izvestia tournament. Many thought the experiment was doomed to failure, as he looked very fragile on ice, but the young sportsman developed his character through hard work.

In the spring of 1981, Andre participated in the world championships in Europe and Sweden. Everyone is aware that he is a master of high calibre who will not evade a strong attack.

Today he is one of the renowned forwards of Soviet hockey, whose courage has been rewarded with awards and medals.

Vyacheslav Fetisov

Vyacheslav Fetisov was born on April 20, 1958 in Moscow. He started hockey as a child at the Central Army sport school and later entered the master team of this club.

Specialists noticed early the talented youth — his speed, style and athletics. At 17, in the ranks of a select team, he won his first gold medal in the European championships, and at 19 was in the ranks of the first select team of the USSR at the World Championships in Vienna. In 1978, in Prague at the championship game he was declared the best player. He achieved similar successes in championship games in 1982, 1985, and 1986, thus catching up to Vladimir Tretiak in awards.

Fetisov was captain of the select USSR hockey team. He scored many goals, but even more goals were scored through his accurate and surprise passes.

In the 1989–90 season, Vyacheslav joined the professional NHL New Jersey Devils team.

For his contribution to Soviet hockey Vyacheslav Fetisov was awarded the Order of Lenin.

Igor Larionov

Igor Larionov was born on December 3, 1960 in Voskresensk, Moscow region. Trainers of local clubs noticed his unusual plays and began to develop his abilities further. Igor successfully defended the honor of his country in the ranks of midget and junior selected teams of the USSR in world and European championships. He began joining championship USSR teams, including the Central Army team, when he was 18.

His amazing coordinated movements and highly technical plays allow this remarkable master to receive a pass at high speed and continue the attack. With keen and unforeseen passes, he aids the forward wings in scoring.

After the world championships in Europe in 1982, Larionov became an indispensable member of the all-union and international tournaments. Sports journalists acknowledged Larionov as the best hockey player in the USSR in the 1987–88 season.

In 1989–90 Igor joined the professional NHL Vancouver Canucks team.

For his advancement of Soviet sport, Igor Larionov has been awarded numerous state medals.

ON THE ICE

```
Y  T  L  A  N  E  P  T
C  W  F  W  I  N  I  S
U  R  I  N  K  E  H  I
P  E  N  E  T  S  R  S
K  F  A  C  O  E  O  S
C  E  L  I  H  R  N  A
U  R  S  C  S  O  I  P
P  E  N  H  L  C  M  A
D  E  F  E  N  S  E  D
B  H  C  A  O  C  A  S
```

Pads	Ice	Minor	Assist
Win	Defense	Referee	Tie
Finals	Penalty	Puck	Coach
Net	Shot	Cup	Rink
Scores	Bench	NHL	

We've hidden the 19 hockey words shown above — written forwards or backwards — in this word search puzzle, placing them either vertically, horizontally, or diagonally. Try and find them! Some letters are used in more than one word.

AND THE WINNER IS . . .

While every player dreams of skating around the ice holding the Stanley Cup over his head, there are some other nice individual trophies to be won as well. See if you can match up the names of the trophies with the reason they are given.

Calder	Best defensive forward
Hart	Most points in regular season
Clancy	League's most valuable player
Ross	Best goalie
Norris	Goalkeeper(s) with fewest goals against
Adams	Rookie of the year
Jennings	Most valuable player in playoffs
Masterton	Best coach
Conn Smythe	Most dedicated and persevering player
Vezina	Most sportsmanlike
Selke	Leadership plus charitable off-ice interests
Lady Byng	Best defenceman

PUZZLING PICTURES

See if you can figure out what these pictures are all about.

___ _____

____ ___

_____ _____

___ ____

31

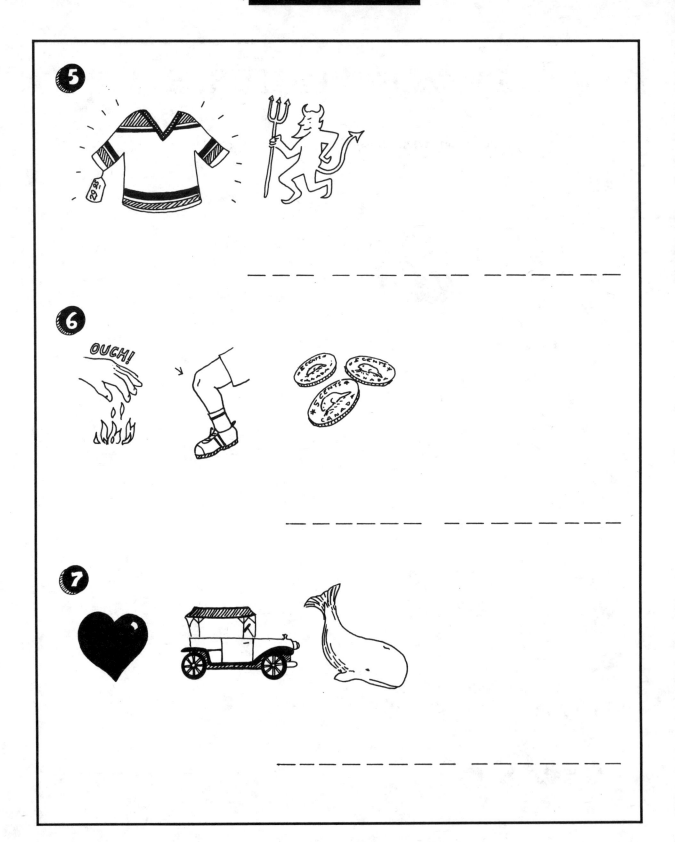

WHO SAID IT?

Most hockey players are known for their actions, not their words. But sometimes something wonderful comes out. See if you can match who said it with what was said.

1 "You would have to have a pretty long stick to score if you spent all your time in the penalty box."

❑ a) Stan Mikita
❑ b) Wayne Gretzky
❑ c) Wendel Clark

2 "When I was a little boy, I used to watch him (Guy LaFleur) on television — next thing you know, I'm sitting beside him. It's amazing."

❑ a) Bernie Nicholls
❑ b) Larry Robinson
❑ c) Joe Sakic

3 "It's a constant, uncompromising struggle. Quite often (in the Soviet League) you could easily predict in advance that the game will be easy. There's no such thing in the NHL."

❑ a) Igor Larionov
❑ b) Alexander Mogilny
❑ c) Zarley Zalapski

4 "You can't doubt yourself. If you doubt yourself, you'll lose."

❑ a) Brett Hull
❑ b) Grant Fuhr
❑ c) Gordie Howe

5 "We played hockey because we loved it. Anything we got paid was considered a bonus."

❑ a) Don Cherry
❑ b) Rocket Richard
❑ c) Rick Tocchet

6 "Hockey is so much *fun!*"

❑ a) John Ziegler
❑ b) Don Koharski
❑ c) Wayne Gretzky

7 Who originally said, "He shoots! He scores!"

❑ a) Foster Hewitt
❑ b) Harold Ballard
❑ c) Dick Irvin

33

RADICAL STATS!

You know what regular stats are like. The kind you turn to as often as you can lay your hands on the sports page, or a copy of *The Hockey News*. Let's see, there are goals, assists, points and penalty minutes, plus power-play, short handed, and game-winning goals. And sometimes there's the plus/minus rating and shooting percentages.

But are you ready for some radical stats? We hope so! And if you come up with some radical stats of your own, drop us a line to the address at the front of the book and we'll consider using them in our next edition.

Most Popular Names!

Yes, we admit it — this is one crazy stat. We searched through the names of the 725 different players who played at least one game in the 1989–90 regular season to find out which names were currently the most popular. And, while we didn't find many of the great old-time names like Aubrey, Hobart, Silas, Sprague, Ferdinand or Montagu (all members of the Hockey Hall of Fame), we did count more than 175 different first names.

We've listed the 20 most popular names. But — as Brett, Trevor, Sergei, Theoren, Mario and Wayne have shown us — it obviously doesn't matter what your name is, it's how you play the game that really counts.

Name	Players With Same Name	Name	Players With Same Name
Mike	30	Paul	12
Dave	24	Tom	11
Bob	19	Craig	10
Mark	18	Jeff	10
Jim	17	Scott	10
Brian	16	Greg	9
John	15	Ken	9
Randy	13	Rob	9
Chris	12	Kevin	8
Doug	12	Ron	8

RADICAL STATS!

Put Me in, Coach — I'm Ready to Play

We were thinking about all the kids who play hockey, either in pick-up games or organized leagues, on city rinks or country ponds, and about many of us dreaming of playing pro hockey one day — and we got to wondering how many people actually play in the NHL each year. And as we thought about it, we figured that maybe the weaker teams in the league would use more players in an effort to spark their teams while the stronger ones would probably have quite solid lineups.

Well, we were partly right! Quebec, who finished last in the 1989-90 season, used the most players — 41, a number which included six goalies, also a league high. But Boston, who finished number one overall, used the second most — 40, with only two goalies — the dynamic duo of Rejean Lemelin and Andy Moog. And Vancouver, who finished in twentieth spot, used only 31 players, while Buffalo, who finished 34 points ahead of them, used 38 players.

In total, 725 different skaters played at least one game during the regular season, with the average number per team, including goalies, being 34. So — keep practising! Especially since NHL expansion is coming and even more players will be needed.

Here are the stats — see if you can make some sense out of them.

Regular Season Standings	# Points	# Players Used
1 Boston	101	40
2 Calgary	99	31
3 Buffalo	98	38
4 Montreal	93	32
5 Edmonton	90	35
6 Chicago	88	31
7 Winnipeg	85	31
8 Hartford	85	34
9 New York Rangers	85	32
10 St. Louis	83	33
11 New Jersey	83	31
12 Toronto	80	35
13 Washington	78	40
14 Minnesota	76	36
15 Los Angeles	75	34
16 New York Islanders	73	35
17 Pittsburgh	72	30
18 Philadelphia	71	38
19 Detroit	70	37
20 Vancouver	64	31
21 Quebec	31	41

RADICAL STATS!

Ironmen

We all know it's a long season, especially when you think that it takes the NHL 80 games to eliminate only five teams and get on with the real season — the playoffs. And when you consider how fast they skate and how hard they hit, you realize that it takes a special kind of person to play in all 80 games.

In the 1989–90 regular season, only 48 players managed to play in all the games. These included Steve Larmer, the Chicago winger who has now played more than eight consecutive NHL seasons (640+ games), though he's still got a ways to go to catch Ironman Doug Jarvis who played a total of 962 games in a row for Montreal, Washington and Hartford from October 8, 1975 to April 5, 1987.

Philadelphia and Detroit were the only two teams without any 80-game players, and Washington led the league with five who listened to the national anthems each night. Many of those who went the distance were among their teams' top point-getters, with nine of them leading their teams. Hartford and Minnesota each had their first-, second-, and fourth-best scorers play all the games.

And what about this discovery — four of the 48 were brothers! Paul and Gino Cavallini of the St. Louis Blues, and Russ Courtnall of Montreal and his brother Geoff of the Capitals.

Here's the complete list of Ironmen with their place in team scoring in brackets behind their name.

Team	Players
Boston	Bob Carpenter (4th)
Buffalo	Pierre Turgeon (1st), Phil Housley (3rd), Dave Snuggerud (10th), Dean Kennedy (18th)
Calgary	Sergei Makarov (4th), Theoren Fleury (8th), Paul Ranheim (9th)
Chicago	Steve Larmer (1st), Adam Creighton (5th)
Detroit	None
Edmonton	Craig Simpson (6th), Craig MacTavish (7th)
Hartford	Ron Francis (1st), Pat Verbeek (2nd), Scott Young (4th)
Los Angeles	Luc Robitaille (2nd)
Minnesota	Brian Bellows (1st), Neal Broten (2nd), Mike Modano (4th), Stewart Gavin (11th)
Montreal	Russ Courtnall (3rd)
New Jersey	Kirk Muller (1st), John MacLean (2nd)
N.Y. Islanders	Doug Crossman (3rd), Dave Volek (9th)
N.Y. Rangers	John Ogrodnick (3rd), Mark Janssens (14th)
Philadelphia	None
Pittsbrugh	Paul Coffey (2nd), Rob Brown (4th)
Quebec	Joe Sakic (1st)
St. Louis	Brett Hull (1st), Adam Oates (2nd), Paul Cavallini (8th), Gino Cavallini (9th)
Toronto	Gary Leeman (1st), Vincent Damphousse (2nd), Rob Ramage (8th), Lou Franceschetti (10th)
Vancouver	Doug Lidster (8th), Garth Butcher (14th)
Washington	Dino Ciccarelli (1st), Geoff Courtnall (2nd), Dale Hunter (5th), Kevin Hatcher (6th), Kelly Miller (7th)
Winnipeg	Pat Elynuik (2nd), Dave McLlwain (6th), Paul Fenton (7th)

IRONMEN TEAM STREAKS

It is interesting to note, again, that often the teams' top Ironmen are also among their top scorers — for example, John Bucyk in Boston, Steve Larmer in Chicago, Wayne Gretzky in Edmonton, Marcel Dionne in Los Angeles, and Dale Hawerchuk in Winnipeg.

Team	Player	Consecutive Games Played	
Boston	John Bucyk	418	1969–1975
Buffalo	Craig Ramsay	776	1973–1983
Calgary	Brad Marsh	257	1978–1981
Chicago	Steve Larmer	640+	1982–199?
Detroit	Alex Delvecchio	548	1956–1964
Edmonton	Wayne Gretzky	362	1979–1984
Hartford	Dave Tippett	419	1984–1989
Los Angeles	Marcel Dionne	324	1978–1982
Minnesota	Danny Grant	442	1968–1974
Montreal	Doug Jarvis	560	1975–1982
New Jersey	Aaron Broten	308	1982–1986
N.Y. Islanders	Bill Harris	576	1972–1979
N.Y. Rangers	Andy Hebenton	560	1955–1963
Philadelphia	Rick MacLeish	287	1972–1976
Pittsburgh	Ron Schock	320	1973–1977
Quebec	Dale Hunter	312	1980–1984
St. Louis	Garry Unger	662	1971–1979
Toronto	Tim Horton	486	1961–1968
Vancouver	Don Lever	437	1972–1978
Washington	Bob Carpenter	422	1981–1987
Winnipeg	Dale Hawerchuk	475	1982–1989

HOCKEY HALL OF FAME

If you like hockey, you'll love the Hockey Hall of Fame in Toronto. It's got game-worn hockey sweaters from current stars like Brett Hull, Steve Yzerman and Mario Lemieux combined with 100-year-old sticks and skates from the game's earliest stars. And there's a complete Gretzky section that includes his first pair of skates and a gold-plated stick given to him by his Oiler teammates when he broke Gordie Howe's assist record of 1050 points.

A special part of the museum has all the NHL trophies on display. The major ones, like the Calder, Norris, Selke and Conn Smythe, are huge; some over three feet tall. And the Vezina trophy for best goaltender even has a miniature net mounted on it.

The video room shows non-stop highlights including the greatest hits, goals, and goalies, plus thrilling overtime victories, Stanley Cup and Canada Cup triumphs.

One of the best displays is a collection of 52 goaltenders' masks that include Jacques Plante's first game-worn mask from 1959, Gilles Gratton's jungle masks, and Grant Fuhr's mask from 1985. There's also a sampling of old pads and early goalie gear from netminding legends Roger Crozier, Terry Sawchuk, Johnny Bower and Ken Dryden.

A section on the NHL expansion years shows jerseys from the defunct Oakland Seals, Kansas City Scouts and Cleveland Barons. And on the walls are photographs and paintings of great hockey players — men and women, amateur and professional — from all over the world.

There's even a Nintendo hockey game — "Blades of Steel" — in the lobby. The Hall of Fame is open year-round; being there is like being in Hockey Heaven.

WHO AM I?

These drawings represent the last names of seven NHL players. We've given you a few hints for their first names. Can you guess who they are?

L _ R _ _   _ _ _ _ _ _ _

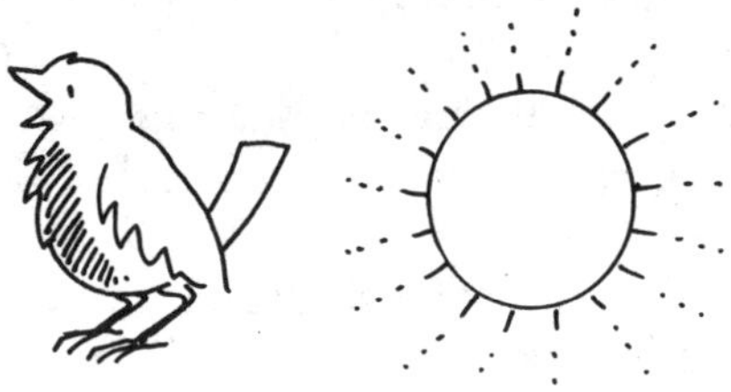

_ A _ T H   _ _ _ _ _ _ _

_ _ _ L   _ _ _ _ _ _

H _ _ R _ N   _ _ _ _ _ _ _

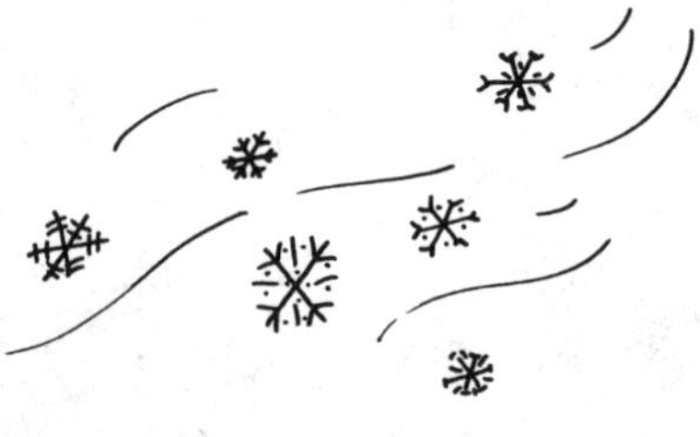

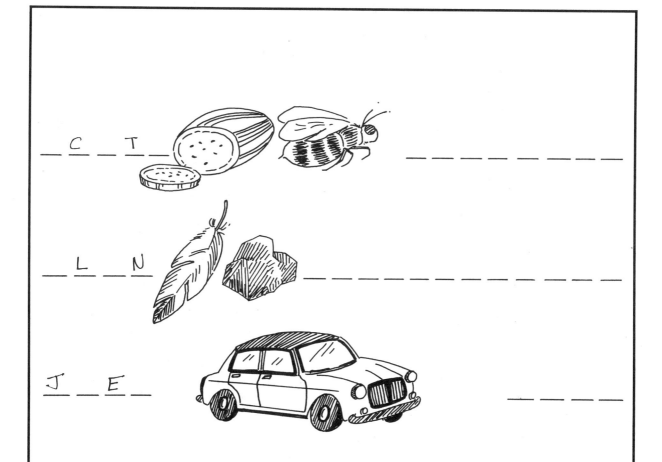

_ C _ T _ _ _ _ _ _ _ _ _ _ _ _ _

_ L _ N _ _ _ _ _ _ _ _ _ _

J _ E _ _ _ _ _ _

Did You Know the L.A. Kings Signed Stephane Richer?

No, we don't mean Stephane Richer, the star right winger who scored 51 goals for Montreal in the 1989–90 season. There is another Stephane Richer, a promising defenceman with the middle initials J. G., who played the last three years in the Montreal organization with the Sherbrooke Canadiens of the American Hockey League.

Richer, the defenceman, came first. He was born on April 23, 1966, in Hull Quebec, while Richer, the winger, came 45 days later in Buckingham, Quebec, approximately 30 miles away. They both weigh 200 pounds, although the Habs winger is three inches taller.

Well, at least now there won't be two Stephane Richers on one team!

WHERE AM I?

In which NHL arena or city would you be if:

1 Twenty-three Stanley Cup banners were hanging above you?

_____

2 Since entering the league in 1970–71, your team had achieved only two winning seasons?

_____

3 There was a giant statue of a superstar in front of your Coliseum?

_____

4 You were watching a Stanley Cup playoff game and the lights went off in your arena for the second time in three years?

_____

5 All announcements over the public address system were in both French and English?

_____

6 Hockey teams in your city had won nine Stanley Cups before 1930, and you were still waiting for an NHL franchise?

_____

7 After being down 5–0 in the early going, fans became so angry with their team's poor showing that they threw rolls of toilet paper (taken from the rink's washrooms) onto the ice, delaying the game for half an hour?

_____

8 You were watching an NHL game in December and some of the fans were wearing T-shirts and shorts?

_____

9 You were watching NHL games in a rink that hockey games in the 1988 Olympics were played in?

_____

OLD-TIMER'S QUIZ

1 Which all-star goalie got so nervous that he threw up before every single game he played — sometimes even between periods?

❑ a) Terry Sawchuk
❑ b) Glenn Hall
❑ c) Jacques Plante

2 Which player in NHL history played all six positions in one hockey game?

❑ a) King Clancy
❑ b) Gordie Howe
❑ c) Howie Morenz

3 Who was perhaps the lightest player who ever played in the NHL?

❑ a) Eddie Shore
❑ b) King Clancy
❑ c) Henri "The Pocket Rocket" Richard

4 Which player fought his way to over 250 penalty minutes in his first two years, and then went on to win the Lady Byng trophy for good behavior?

❑ a) Bobby Orr
❑ b) Dave Schultz
❑ c) Stan Mikita

5 Which player scored the fastest hat trick in NHL history? (21 seconds)

❑ a) Sid Abel
❑ b) Bill Mosienko
❑ c) Jean Beliveau

6 The "Kid Line" is currently racking up points for the Edmonton Oilers. On which 1930s team did the original "Kid Line" of Charlie Conacher, Harvey Jackson and Joe Primeau play?

❑ a) Toronto Maple Leafs
❑ b) Chicago Blackhawks
❑ c) Montreal Maroons

Do you have what it takes to make the All-Rookie team? Give it a try — you might even become Rookie of the Year! For this game, you will need a marker for each player, plus one die. Start at square #1 and end on #40. Good luck!

You score your 40th goal!! Go ahead 1.

You are named Rookie of the Year!

...And your fellow teammates in this game make the ALL ROOKIE TEAM!

37 38 39 40

You accidentally score on your own goal. Go back 2.

ARGHH!

You are the leading Rookie goal scorer. Go ahead 2.

Hi Mom!

28 27 26 25

You slept in and the team left without you! Miss a turn.

ZZZ

21 22 23 24

You get creamed and sprain your ankle. Miss a turn.

12 11 10 9

You make the team! Go ahead 3.

5 6 7 8

ALLSTAR HOCKEY

DEGRACE '90

ANSWERS

Nicknames - Page 6

Wayne Gretzky – The Great One
Larry Robinson – Big Bird
Terry Sawchuk – Mr. Zero
Mark Messier – Mess
Yvan Cournoyer – Roadrunner
Frank Brimsek – Mr. Zero (the original)
Richard Brodeur – King Richard
Dave Schultz – The Hammer
Rick Middleton – Nifty
Glen Sather – Slats
Guy Lafleur – Flower
Stan Smyl – Steamer
Dave Williams – Tiger
Garry Unger – Ironman
Gordie Howe – Mr. Hockey
Maurice Richard – Rocket
Henri Richard – Pocket Rocket
Bernie Geoffrion – Boom Boom
Don Cherry – Grapes
Ken Linseman – Rat

Are You Kidding? - Page 8

1. c) rubber
2. a) red
3. b) toilet paper rolls
4. c) Foster Hewitt
5. b) lacrosse
6. a) knights
7. b) the power went out and lights
    went off
8. a) Dale Hawerchuk
9. b) Dawson Nuggets
10. b) the zamboni crashed through the
    ice and sunk
11. b) Peter Stastny
12. d) all of the above
13. c) Helmut Balderis
14. b) his leg was accidentally broken
15. a) Grant Fuhr
16. c) so it would show up on black
    and white television
17. b) because of his habit of yanking
    goalies

100-Point Scorers - Page 17

Lemieux Coffey

Who Am I? - Page 18

Rick Lanz

Gone But Not Forgotten - Page 19

Buffalo #11 - Gilbert Perreault; Toronto #6 - Ace Bailey; St. Louis #11 - Brian Sutter; Boston #4 - Bobby Orr; Calgary #9 - Lanny McDonald; Detroit #9 - Gordie Howe; Boston #7 - Phil Esposito; Winnipeg #9 - Bobby Hull; Chicago #35 - Tony Esposito; Los Angeles #30 - Rogatien Vachon; Minnesota #19 - Bill Masterton; Chicago #1 - Glenn Hall; Montreal #10 - Guy Lafleur; Rangers #7 - Rod Gilbert; Philadelphia #16 - Bobby Clarke; Montreal #9 - Maurice Richard; Buffalo #2 - Tim Horton; Quebec #3 - J. C. Tremblay.

ANSWERS

When Did They Start? - Page 20

Boston Bruins 1924–25; Buffalo Sabres 1970–71; Calgary Flames 1980–81; Chicago Blackhawks 1926–27; Detroit Red Wings 1926–27; Edmonton Oilers 1979–80; Hartford Whalers 1979–80; Los Angeles Kings 1967–68; Minnesota North Stars 1967-68; Montreal Canadiens 1917–18; New Jersey Devils 1974–75; New York Islanders 1972–73; New York Rangers 1926–27; Philadephia Flyers 1967–68; Pittsburgh Penguins 1967–68; Quebec Nordiques 1979–80; St. Louis Blues 1967–68; Toronto Maple Leafs 1917–18; Vancouver Canucks 1970–71; Washington Capitals 1974–75; Winnipeg Jets 1979–80.

Where Were They Born? - Page 21

Uwe Krupp – West Germany
Joe Mullen – United States
Steve Thomas – Great Britain
Trevor Linden – Canada
Rod Langway – Taiwan
Peter Sidorkiewicz – Poland
Paul MacLean – France
Rick Lanz – Czechoslovakia
Anatoli Semenov – Soviet Union
Robert Nordmark – Sweden
Mikko Makela – Finland

On the Ice - Page 29

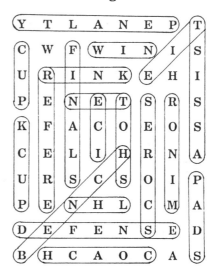

And the Winner Is - Page 30

Calder – Rookie of the year
Hart – League's most valuable player
Clancy – Leadership plus charitable off-ice interests
Ross – Most points in regular season
Norris – Best defenceman
Adams – Best coach
Jennings – Goalkeeper(s) with fewest goals against
Masterton – Most dedicated and persevering player
Conn Smyth – Most valuable player in playoffs
Vezina – Best goalie
Selke – Best defensive forward
Lady Byng – Most sportsmanlike

ANSWERS

Puzzling Pictures - Page 31

1. Don Cherry
2. Face off
3. North Stars
4. Jim Kite
5. New Jersey Devils
6. Bernie Nicholls
7. Hartford Whalers

Who Said It? - Page 33

1. a) Stan Mikita
2. c) Joe Sakic
3. a) Igor Larionov
4. b) Grant Fuhr
5. b) Rocket Richard
6. c) Wayne Gretzky
7. a) Foster Hewitt

Who Am I? - Page 40

Larry Robinson
Garth Butcher
Paul Coffey
Theoren Fleury
Scott Mellanby
Glen Featherstone
Joel Otto

Where Am I? - Page 42

1. Montreal
2. Vancouver
3. Edmonton
4. Boston
5. Montreal
6. Ottawa
7. Quebec City
8. Los Angeles
9. Calgary

Old-Timers Quiz - Page 43

1. b) Glenn Hall
2. a) King Clancy
3. b) King Clancy
4. c) Stan Mikita
5. b) Bill Mosienko
6. a) Toronto Maple Leafs